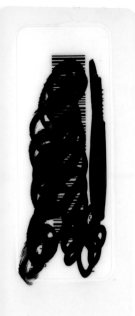

Brazil

by Grace Hansen

Abdo
COUNTRIES
Kids

Abdo Kids Jumbo is an Imprint of Abdo Kids
abdobooks.com

abdobooks.com

Published by Abdo Kids, a division of ABDO, P.O. Box 398166, Minneapolis, Minnesota 55439.
Copyright © 2020 by Abdo Consulting Group, Inc. International copyrights reserved in all countries.
No part of this book may be reproduced in any form without written permission from the publisher.
Abdo Kids Jumbo™ is a trademark and logo of Abdo Kids.

Printed in the United States of America, North Mankato, Minnesota.

052019

092019

Photo Credits: Alamy, Getty Images, iStock, Shutterstock, ©AP/Shutterstock p.9

Production Contributors: Teddy Borth, Jennie Forsberg, Grace Hansen
Design Contributors: Dorothy Toth, Pakou Moua

Library of Congress Control Number: 2018963334
Publisher's Cataloging-in-Publication Data

Names: Hansen, Grace, author.
Title: Brazil / by Grace Hansen.
Description: Minneapolis, Minnesota : Abdo Kids, 2020 | Series: Countries |
    Includes online resources and index.
Identifiers: ISBN 9781532185496 (lib. bdg.) | ISBN 9781532186479 (ebook) |
    ISBN 9781532186967 (Read-to-me ebook)
Subjects: LCSH: Brazil--Juvenile literature. | Brazil--History--Juvenile
    literature. | Latin America--Juvenile literature. | Geography--Juvenile literature.
Classification: DDC 981--dc23

Table of Contents

Brazil's History

Brazil is a country in South America. American Indians were the first people to live there. In 1500, **Pedro Álvares Cabral** landed on the coast of Brazil. He claimed the land for Portugal.

North
America

Portugal —

Africa

Pacific
Ocean

Brazil

Atlantic
Ocean

South
America

N

W E

S

5

Beginning in the 1690s, many people moved to Brazil. They were in search of riches, like diamonds and gold.

6

7

The country claimed its **independence** from Portugal in 1822. But Portuguese is still the country's official language.

Geography & Major Cities

Ten countries border Brazil. The Atlantic Ocean borders the east side of the country. The capital of Brazil is Brasília. It is home to more than 2.8 million people.

Venezuela

Guyana

Suriname

French Guiana

Colombia

Ecuador

Amazon River

Brazil

Peru

Brasília

Bolivia

Pacific
Ocean

São
Paulo

Paraguay

N
W E
S

Argentina

Atlantic
Ocean

Uruguay

Chile

South America

Brazil's largest city is São Paulo. More than 12 million people live there. It is known throughout the world for business, arts, and **entertainment**.

13

Brazil is a beautiful country.

It has mountains, rainforests,

coastline, and more than

1,000 rivers! The Amazon

River is the longest.

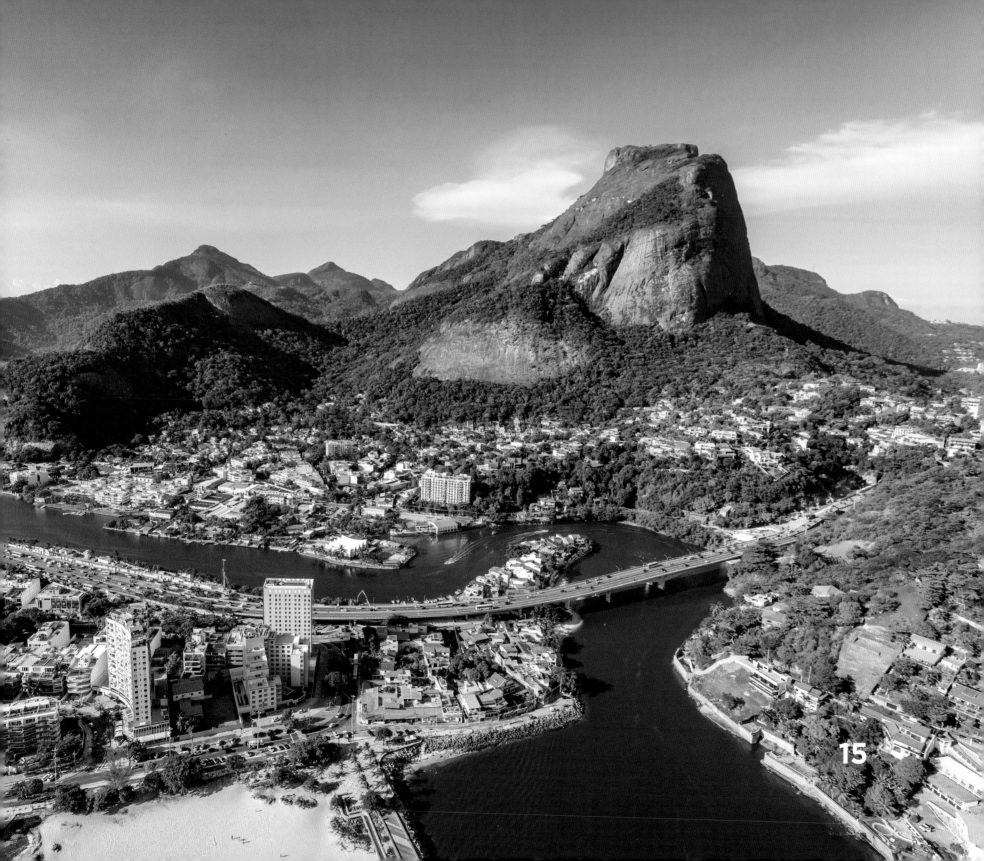

15

Plants & Animals

The Amazon rainforest is in Brazil. It holds more types of plants than any other place on Earth. Anacondas, toucans, jaguars and more make their homes there.

Foods

Common foods include beans, seafood, and rice. Tropical fruits like bananas and coconuts are popular too.

Futebol

Futebol, or soccer, is a favorite sport in Brazil. Pelé is a famous soccer player. He was born in south eastern Brazil in 1940. He scored 77 goals for Brazil's national team!

21

Awesome Landmarks in Brazil

Amazon Theatre
Amazonas, Brazil

Christ the Redeemer
Corcovado Mountain,
Rio de Janeiro, Brazil

Iguazu Falls
Paraná, Brazil

Itaimbezinho Canyon
Santa Catarina, Brazil

Glossary

coastline – the line where land meets water.

entertainment – something that amuses or interests.

independence – freedom from outside control.

Pedro Álvares Cabral – (1467–1520) was a Portuguese noblemen, military commander, navigator, and explorer who is known to be the European discoverer of Brazil.

Index

Abdo Kids
ONLINE
FREE! ONLINE MULTIMEDIA RESOURCES

Visit abdokids.com
to access crafts, games,
videos, and more!

Use Abdo Kids code

CBK5496

or scan this QR code!